COMMUNITIES
HELPING COMMUNITIES
by Erin Ash Sullivan

TABLE OF CONTENTS

INTRODUCTION

People around the world face hard problems. Sometimes there are earthquakes. Sometimes hurricanes hit. Sometimes there are wars.

In some places, children do not have enough to eat. Other children don't have medicine when they are sick. Some children don't have schools.

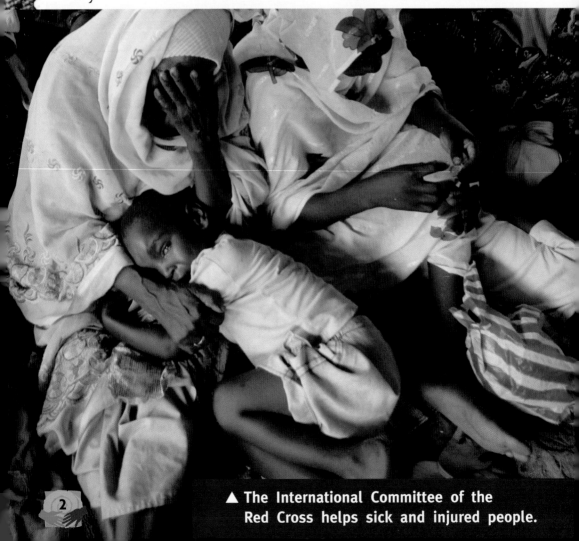

▲ The International Committee of the Red Cross helps sick and injured people.

Even Earth is in trouble. Wild places are disappearing. **Pollution** is hurting the air, the land, and the water. Some wild animals are disappearing.

▲ The World Wildlife Fund helps protect animals in danger.

But there is good news. There are groups that help solve these problems. The groups help when disasters hit. They help children in many ways. Some groups work to save wild animals. Others work to save Earth. Around the world there are communities helping other communities.

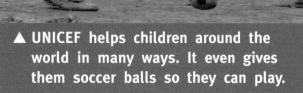

▲ UNICEF helps children around the world in many ways. It even gives them soccer balls so they can play.

THE INTERNATIONAL COMMITTEE OF
THE RED CROSS

In 2001, a volcano erupted in the Philippines. People ran for cover. Thousands needed help. The International Committee of the Red Cross came. They brought medicine, food, and water.

▲ Nearly 47,000 people lost their homes when a volcano erupted in the Philippines.

The International Committee of the Red Cross is an **organization**, or group. It was started in 1863. Most people call this group the Red Cross.

The Red Cross helps people everywhere. It helps when there are disasters, such as volcanoes or earthquakes. It also helps when there are wars.

One thing makes the Red Cross special. It is neutral. That means it doesn't take sides. The Red Cross helps anyone who is hurt, hungry, or homeless. If there is a war, the Red Cross helps people on both sides.

▲ **This Red Cross poster was created in 1939.**

1. SOLVE THIS

Many Red Cross organizations have blood drives. People donate blood to help other people who are sick or hurt. The average adult has about 10 pints (4.7 liters) of blood in his or her body. A person who donates blood gives about 1 pint. How could you show the amount of donated blood as a fraction?

Math ✓ Point Is your answer reasonable? Why or why not?

WAR IN EUROPE

In 1999, there was a war in Kosovo (KOH-soh-voh). Kosovo was a province, or region, of Serbia. Many people lost their homes. They had nowhere to go. They had no blankets or warm clothes. Thousands of people became **refugees** (REH-fyoo-jeez). They were forced to leave their homes.

▲ Kosovo is in Eastern Europe

▲ Hundreds of thousands of people from Kosovo were driven from their homes into refugee camps.

The Red Cross went there to help. **Volunteers** gave out tents, sleeping bags, and blankets. They brought food. They brought milk powder to make milk for babies.

The Red Cross couldn't bring peace to the people of Kosovo, but it did bring them food, warmth, and hope.

They Made a Difference

In 1859, a Swiss man named Henry Dunant (doo-NAHNT) watched a battle. He was upset that no one was helping the injured soldiers. He decided to get doctors and nurses to help all soldiers, no matter what side they fought on. That was the start of the Red Cross.

 Point   Visualize

Imagine yourself as a refugee in Kosovo. What do you see yourself doing to pass the time? What do you see yourself doing to help your family?

EARTHQUAKE IN ASIA

It was October of 2005. People in the Asian region of Kashmir (KASH-meer) were enjoying a quiet night. Then, suddenly, the ground shook. It was an earthquake!

▲ Kashmir is a region in Asia. It borders India, China, and Pakistan.

The earthquake was one of the largest in history. Villages were destroyed. Many people were lost or trapped in mountain areas.

▲ This girl was one of the lucky ones. She survived the earthquake in Kashmir.

The Red Cross came to the rescue. Doctors, nurses, and other volunteers flew to Kashmir.

The volunteers set up hospitals. It was not easy. Kashmir had few good roads. In many places there was no running water or electricity. But a hospital needs those things. The Red Cross put up hospital tents. They used batteries for power. They brought fresh water. At last the sick and hurt people could get help.

▲ Earthquakes can do a lot of damage in just a few minutes.

Careers

Doctors Without Borders

Many doctors from all over the world are part of a group called Doctors Without Borders. They fly to places where there is a disaster. They help people who are sick or hurt. Like the Red Cross, members of Doctors Without Borders are neutral. They do not get paid for their work. They help people because they care.

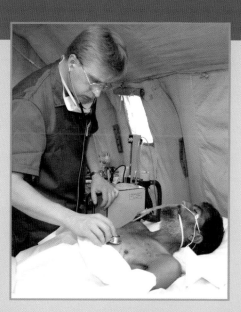

UNICEF

In 2000, there was a serious **drought** (DROWT) in Africa. It didn't rain for months. Families in many countries lost their crops. Farm animals died. People were hungry and sick. UNICEF was there to help.

UNICEF is an organization that helps children around the world. It sends doctors to help children stay healthy. It sets up schools. It works for laws that keep children safe.

Historical Perspective

Trick or Treat for UNICEF

Have you ever taken one of these with you on Halloween? UNICEF made these orange boxes in the 1950s so that children could collect money for other children in need. Today, American children collect millions of dollars for UNICEF to help kids.

It's a Fact

In many countries around the world, girls do not have the same chances in life that boys do. Some countries don't want girls to go to school. UNICEF works hard to see that girls get a good education. They make sure girls are treated fairly.

UNICEF began in 1946. A war left many children in Europe without homes or food. At that time, the United Nations had just been started. It is an organization that helps countries work together to solve problems. The United Nations decided that it needed a special group of people to deal with the problems of children. So they created UNICEF. The letters stand for "United Nations Children's Fund."

HELPING CHILDREN STAY HEALTHY

One of UNICEF's most important jobs is to help children stay healthy. Children in many countries do not get enough food. Sometimes there is no rain. Crops can't grow. Without crops, there isn't enough food. Wars can also stop people from growing enough food.

▲ In some villages in India, it is hard to find fresh water. UNICEF helps by making sure people have water pumps.

Children need good food and clean water to grow up healthy. UNICEF sends help. Sometimes workers give out food and vitamins. They also set up water pumps for clean, fresh water.

UNICEF also makes sure that children get **immunizations** (ih-myuh-nih-ZAY-shunz). The shots of medicine keep children safe from disease. The shots help save lives each year.

2. SOLVE THIS

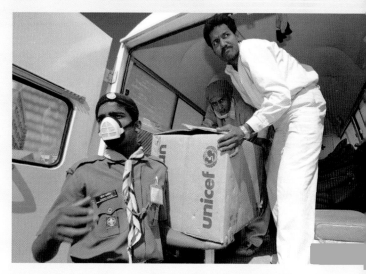

UNICEF helped children in Afghanistan (af-GA-nih-stan). During the cold winters, workers gave out 800,000 blankets. They gave out 730,000 winter clothes. They gave out 500,000 socks and boots. How many items were handed out in all?

Math ✓ Point

Is your answer reasonable? Why or why not?

PLAY IS IMPORTANT

What if you could not go to school? What if you couldn't play during the day? Some children around the world have no time to go to school or play. They must work. Some start working when they are four.

UNICEF believes that every child should go to school and have time to play. UNICEF works to change laws about **child labor**, or work done by children.

✓ Point   Think About It

Most of this chapter is about problems such as hunger and poor health. Why did the author think it was important to include information about play?

▲ UNICEF wants all children to be able to play.

UNICEF also believes that sports are important. Sports help children to be healthy and strong. Sports teach children how to work in teams. But in some poor countries, children can't afford sports equipment. UNICEF helps. It sends the children special boxes. Inside each "Sport-in-a-Box" kit, children find everything they need to play a game of soccer.

▲ UNICEF is trying to stop child labor. Some children work in factories like this.

3. SOLVE THIS

UNICEF sent out 100 Sport-in-a-Box kits to 12 different countries. How many boxes did they send in all?

Math ✓ Point How could you check your work?

CHAPTER 3

THE WORLD WILDLIFE FUND

The Amazon Rain Forest is an amazing place. All kinds of animals and plants live there. Jaguars prowl the rain forest floor. Two-toed sloths hang from trees. Harpy eagles soar overhead. But the rain forest is in danger. The animals that live there are in danger, too. Who will save the rain forest and the creatures that call it home? The World Wildlife Fund (WWF) is an important organization that is working to save the rain forest.

▲ The toucan is just one of the many animals that live in the Amazon Rain Forest.

The World Wildlife Fund has three goals. It works to save animals that are **endangered** (in-DANE-jerd). These animals are in danger of becoming **extinct** (ik-STINGKT), or dying out completely. The WWF also works to protect **habitats**, the places where animals and plants live. And the World Wildlife Fund works to stop pollution.

The World Wildlife Fund has a hard job. Many animals are in danger. Many parts of Earth suffer from pollution. But WWF volunteers work hard to keep Earth and its animals and plants safe.

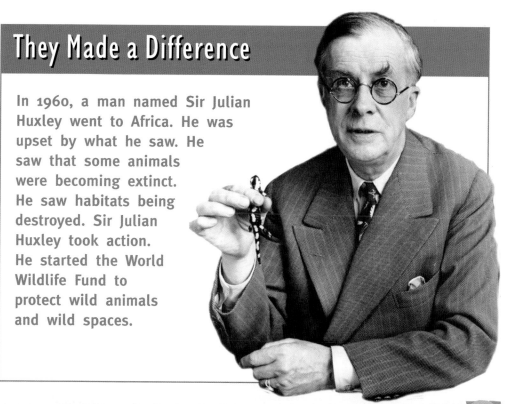

They Made a Difference

In 1960, a man named Sir Julian Huxley went to Africa. He was upset by what he saw. He saw that some animals were becoming extinct. He saw habitats being destroyed. Sir Julian Huxley took action. He started the World Wildlife Fund to protect wild animals and wild spaces.

SAVING SPECIES

Have you ever seen a dodo? Or a Carolina parakeet? You haven't because they're extinct. Those species of birds are gone from Earth forever.

The World Wildlife Fund works hard to protect endangered animals. Some animals become endangered because humans take over their habitats. Some animals are hunted too much. Sometimes diseases cause many animals to die.

▲ Long ago, farmers thought Carolina parakeets were pests. So they hunted the birds. Eventually, the species died out.

▲ Very few rhinos live in the wild today. Most of them live on safe lands called nature reserves.

One animal the World Wildlife Fund wants to save is the rhinoceros. There used to be many rhinos. They lived in Africa and Asia. Then hunters started killing too many rhinos, and not many were left. What does the WWF do to help? It works to stop people from hunting the rhinos. It works to set aside land that is safe for rhinos. The plan is working. Now the rhino population is growing.

4. SOLVE THIS

The leatherback turtle is endangered. The World Wildlife Fund is trying to save this special animal. Over the past few years, more leatherback turtles have built their nests along the coast of Florida.

Look at this graph. About how many nests were there in 1997? How many in 2003? How many more were there in 2003 than in 1997?

Math ✓ Point

What steps did you follow to get your answers?

Leatherback Turtle Nests
1997–2004

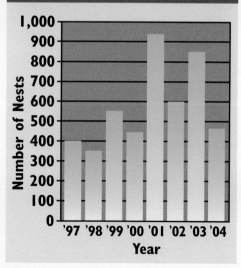

SAVING HABITATS

The World Wildlife Fund works hard to protect habitats. When animal homes are safe, the animals are safe.

The rain forest of South America is one of the most important habitats on Earth. Many kinds of plants and animals can be found only in the rain forest.

▲ If the WWF is successful in protecting the Amazon Rain Forest, the protected habitats there will be larger than the entire national park system of the United States!

How is the World Wildlife Fund working to keep the rain forest safe? It created a plan to protect almost 200,000 square miles (518,000 square kilometers) of rain forest.

So far, the plan is working. In Brazil, you can find Tumucumaque (too-moo-koo-MAH-kay) Mountains National Park. It is the largest tropical forest national park in the world. The animals and plants that live there are safe.

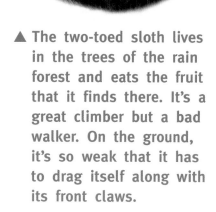

▲ The two-toed sloth lives in the trees of the rain forest and eats the fruit that it finds there. It's a great climber but a bad walker. On the ground, it's so weak that it has to drag itself along with its front claws.

5. Solve This

One out of every three animal species in the world can be found in the Amazon. Is this closer to 5%, 10%, or 30%?

Math ✔ Point

Is your answer reasonable? Why or why not?

CONCLUSION

There are many problems in the world. Natural disasters happen. In some countries, wars are being fought. People need help. Children are hungry. Animals and habitats need protection.

There are organizations that try to solve those problems. People around the world are working together. Thousands of volunteers work hard every day. They make sure that people get what they need and that Earth is protected. When people work together as a community, they can make a big difference.

Name of Organization	Goals	Where It Works
Red Cross	to help people who are homeless, sick, or injured because of man-made disasters (wars) and because of natural disasters (earthquakes, hurricanes, etc.)	all over the world
UNICEF	to help children by providing healthy food and water, by giving immunizations, and by supporting laws to protect children	all over the world
World Wildlife Fund	to protect Earth by saving endangered species and habitats, and by fighting pollution	all over the world

▲ This chart shows what each organization does.

GLOSSARY

child labor   (CHILD LAY-ber) children being forced to work (page 14)

drought   (DROWT) a long time with no rain (page 10)

endangered   (in-DANE-jerd) threatened with dying out forever (page 17)

extinct   (ik-STINGKT) no longer living anywhere on Earth (page 17)

habitat   (HA-bih-tat) a place where plants and animals live (page 17)

immunization   (ih-myuh-nih-ZAY-shun) shots to protect people from disease (page 13)

organization   (or-guh-nih-ZAY-shun) a group of people joined together for a particular purpose (page 5)

pollution   (puh-LOO-shun) harmful materials that make the air, water, or soil dirty (page 3)

refugee   (REH-fyoo-jee) a person who flees from a place to find safety (page 6)

volunteer   (vah-lun-TEER) someone who helps without pay (page 7)

SOLVE THIS ANSWERS

1. **Page 5** 1 out of 10 pints = 1/10
2. **Page 13** 800,000 + 730,000 + 500,000 = 2,030,000 items
3. **Page 15** 100 boxes x 12 countries = 1,200 boxes
4. **Page 19** about 400 leatherback nests in 1997; about 850 leatherback nests in 2003

   850 − 400 = 450 more leatherback nests counted in 2003
5. **Page 21** 30%

INDEX